How to Market Yourself in a Week

By

Steve Mullins

Published by *Ascot Associates Ltd*

How to Market Yourself in a Week

A step-by-step self-help guide and work-book to help you
- *Find a job,*
- *Change your job*
- *Improve your career*

At little personal cost by using techniques that have been shown to work

This book is written for all those people who:
- Want to progress in their organisation
- Are facing redundancy
- Have been made redundant
- Are looking for a job
- Are just plain fed-up with their current boss or organisation

Based on personal experience with a few helpful appendices

First published in electronic format to Kindle 2013.

Republished in paperback 2015 with revisions and added sections.

The right of Steve Mullins to be identified as the author of this book has been asserted by him in accordance with the Copyright, Design and Patents Act, 1998.

Published by **Ascot Associates Ltd**

ISBN 978-0-9576340-3-9

Contents

How to use this book

Rarely do we think of ourselves as objects or marketable commodities, yet to the employer that is what we are regardless of banal statements about our people are our most valuable asset – just watch what happens in an economic downturn.

In order to be desirable to an employer you need to package yourself as a commodity that will deliver benefits to the hiring organisation and this demands a change of mind-set.

Too often we look out from ourselves at what it is that we want, totally selfish and totally understandable yet an employer has little or no interest in your aspirations, mainly what you can do for the organisation.

Many people need to reverse this process and look critically at themselves from the viewpoint of the employer, establish strengths and weaknesses, recognise what will make them desirable in the prospective employer's eyes and then compete like hell with everyone else who would like that particular job.

The chapters and exercises provided here are designed to make that transition from looking out at what you want to look inwardly to recognise what will make you competitive in a particular job market (the specific vacancy).

Everyone is individual and there is no one right way that works for everyone. This book is written as a journey where you complete the sections in a way that is right for you and your circumstances – not the world in general.

There are five sections; one for each day of the week and each builds logically on the one before it.

Take the time to read the material a day at a time to get a feel for where it's headed and then read it again more carefully, referencing the appendices where appropriate.

After each section there is a short exercise to help you explore the material and what it means to you; the exercise will help you to put the information and ideas into a context that matches your ambition and opportunities.

When moving on to the next day, go back over the material and exercises already completed as they will provide a foundation for the next stage of the journey.

After the five days you should have a personal manual that will take you to market and which will usually benefit at this stage from mature reflection. Take the weekend to go back over the exercises, re-read the appendices, get your mental model just right.

And then: **Attack, Attack, Attack**.

Reasons to write this book

Over many years I've been fired, outplaced, promoted, demoted and head-hunted; in short I have seen, and been subject to, most elements of good, and bad, management.

Latterly I was allowed to put some of this experience to practical use as a member of a team involved in corporate outplacement, where it became evident that people at all levels in an organisation struggle to know what to say, or who to say it to.

My aim is to remove some of the pressure and anguish that I went through as a pawn in corporate life to make progress and new employment much less of the shock and trial than I went through (several times).

In looking for a new job or a promotion, not every applicant will get an interview – that goes without saying, so it's important to recognise that fact and take advantage of some of the methods and ideas discussed in this book to find ways that will help you to:

Get noticed
Show that you're a bit special
Get ahead of the competition
Keep your confidence high
Treat every opportunity seriously.

And that is what this book is written to achieve

A successful interview is life changing

In this short book you'll find some of the techniques and approaches I've used successfully in the past to help people into new work; those people have ranged from progress chasers to international executives.

It's an approach that works at every level of an organisation and whatever your circumstances.

Each section is concluded with a reprise of the material as a simple exercise that you may wish to complete, or to skip, that's your decision; the purpose is to bring the contents of the section to life and provide you with another step on the road to success.

An advantage of completing these brief exercises is that you will have thought through the material and how it relates to you; it will provide a record to go back to when reviewing the progress of your campaign and highlight which bits to work on some more.

You will know which aspects work well and which to develop further in order to provide a plan which also supports continual self-development.

I hope it helps you.

Preface

The economic reality is that organisations need to be able to continue to invest in their own sustainability which, for some, demands cutting back or returning to their core function.

Because of this cutting back, the competition for available jobs is getting progressively fiercer – which is why you have to stand head and shoulders above the rest (1) to be in with a good chance of finding a new job.

Get it right and redundancy can offer new opportunities and improve your lifestyle by finding a fulfilling new direction – as many have found out. If you do nothing or get complacent you'll stay where you are.

This book takes experiences from coaching, mentoring and support programmes normally reserved for senior management and brings them together in one place.

My own background is one of over twenty years in management and, after trying to change some awful systems, have been fired on several occasions as well as being outplaced.

In the end I decided to become self-employed where I've spent over twenty years as a support specialist involved in outplacing people from multinational organisations as well as strategic planning and business mentoring.

There is now so much (sometimes conflicting) material to support people looking to move on that I felt it was time to crystallise some of that into a short, practical book that can act as a first point of reference for people seeking a move to a new job, or position, somewhere better.

That does not preclude your exploring Monster and other on-line sources of jobs, ideas and inspiration – in fact it is recommended to explore as widely as possible to be able to develop an approach and material that is right for you and right for the opportunity on offer.

Some aspects might be obvious to you but will be new to a different reader, conversely stuff that is obvious to them may be new to you.

That said, we often overlook the obvious – and that will be the thing that trips us up at a critical point in the process (Sod's law).

And, on a positive note, my experience when talking to people who have moved to a new job is that all have said it is so much better than the one they have just left

Thank you

Thanks to family and friends for their support, too many to mention you all but in particular (in first name alphabetical order):

• Sister Ann (who is dyslexic like me) for checking readability
• Son Jon for managing the original Kindle stuff
• Niece Lydia for turning it into sensible English
• Son Tom for some quite ruthless editing
• Colleague Vince Golder (MD of Goldnet Referral Marketing) for the list of referral opportunities and leads at appendix 5.

All have been immensely supportive in covering my weaknesses but the content is exclusively mine, so any inaccuracies, errors or fundamental cock-ups are all my responsibility and no-one else's.

Steve Mullins April 2015

Dedications (or a lack of)

The people I should dedicate this book to are those who fired me, outplaced me, manipulated me or just generally pissed me off by their dithering, lack of vision or inability to take responsibility.

But because I do not value sycophants, self-seekers, jobsworths or posers I have decided to minimise this section and concentrate on what really matters – getting you into a better position or back into paid employment.

Now onwards and upwards

Introduction

During my twenty-odd years in industry I was fired several times, head-hunted, outplaced and I even fired myself from a firm that I found quite uncomfortable as it was being managed for political ends (the egos of the few) and not driven for results (the benefit of the many).

Looking back, these were very valuable experiences and have helped to build the resilience I now enjoy to operate as a strategist, support specialist and business mentor; and whilst it might sound out of place as you read this there's nearly always something good that comes from an upset – even though it's not obvious at the time. My personal experience is that this is usually the case.

Over the last twenty-odd years I have been involved in outplacement for major corporations, helped advertise for and employ new staff and counselled people in the process of being 'let go'.

I've also developed a diagnostic for disgruntled senior management to help them better manage their futures.

My qualifications to give advice come from a history of being hired, retired, rotated and fired which has allowed me to understand and have empathy for people looking for a new position.

A distillation of this experience comes down to a number of distinct and logical steps which are covered in the chapters of this book.

In the final analysis, the aim of this book is to give you the tools to package yourself and take you – the shiny new product – to market.

Most probably you have different experiences and alternative ways to go about finding a job, gaining promotion or selling yourself – all in a competitive setting.

Please pick and choose from the material here to add to your own knowledge and understanding to give your approach to market a bit of extra weight.

Please feel free to criticise, proof read, challenge or add to the material in this book by e-mailing me at steve.mullins@virgin.net when any appropriate comments will be included in future editions with thanks and an acknowledgment for you.

Summary

The book is divided into a number of discrete and logical sections that build on one another to provide a rounded package designed to take you to market – the job market.

Monday – Build Your Foundations

Section 1. *The Past Will Not Return*, however much you want to reminisce; you need to let go of the organisation that has dumped you and look to <u>your</u> future – they can look after themselves.

Section 2. *Get Back Your Old Confidence* by taking the time to really get to know yourself again. After having being beaten up for several years, corporate pummelling causes us to build strong defences – even from ourselves; we need to find a way through these defences and become vulnerable once again.

Section 3. *Remind Yourself Who You Really Are* by identifying your good points, useful experiences and transferrable skills – and then check them with other people.

We rarely see ourselves as others see us – sometimes due to the defences we've built; often there's a different person at work to the one at home (2).

Section 4. *Identify the Right Market Sector* – one where your skills and experiences will be properly valued and you can apply that accumulated wisdom and knowledge in a way that is right for you, as well as for the organisation you will be joining.

Tuesday – Get to Know Yourself

Section 5. *Package Yourself as a Product for Market*, identify the tangible benefits that will justify your being hired and those intangible benefits that will build confidence in the interviewer and positively sell you as a person.

Each job is different, so be prepared to emphasise the relevant aspects of your real self in your 'sales pitch'.

Section 6. *Building Your CV* into a document that describes you, your skills and the appropriate benefits you can deliver to a potential employer. There is no perfect CV so don't get too hung up about format.

Wednesday – Get to Know Your Target

Section 7. *Reaching Target Organisations* by appropriately putting yourself in front of the decision-makers after carefully reading the job advert. Many people don't get to interview because they haven't tailored the response to the specifics of the post or the organisation.

Section 8. *Go To Market – Aim High* in a positive and practiced way and work your contacts mercilessly (they may need the favour returned before too long).

Each job is different and may need a different approach. Take every opportunity for interview practice, even consider being coached and don't be shy about applying for jobs that aren't exactly right for you – you'll learn from the experience.

Thursday – Engage

Section 9. *Meet the Interviewer*; the person you first meet may not be the decision-maker and will need to be treated differently from the person who eventually hires or promotes you. Recognising the different types will help you be more persuasive by being able to play to the different styles.

Section 10. *Presentation and Follow-up:* it's a trite comment that *you only have one opportunity to make a first impression* but that first impression can be the difference between winning and losing – however clever you are!

Here are a selection of popular questions that you might be asked and some for you to ask during and after the interview.

Follow-up counts too, it's too easy to send an e-mail that gets ignored – how about a paper letter that has to be opened?

Friday – Control and Some Alternatives

Section 11. *Build Resilience* by examining your performance, monitor and measure how well you're doing to identify those areas where you are strong – it's a long haul and easy to get disheartened, so build on triumphs, treat finding a new job as a project and manage it as such; use your close friends to support you and you may be able to support them later in return.

Section 12. *Going it Alone* explores whether one of the many forms of self-employment might be the right way forward. A decision-tree is provided to ask some of the questions to help you reach a solution that is right for you.

Section 13. *Help, Support and a Note of Caution* looks at support that is available at different prices and at different levels of professionalism. Please seek appropriate and affordable support; there is nothing to gain by being insular and withdrawn or even by seeking the cheapest option.

The **Appendices** provide summaries of some of the more important parts: what constitutes a benefit, ideas for CVs and sources of leads; all designed to help get you in front of the right people with the right approach.

About the Author provides a potted background to Steve.

End Notes are used rather than distracting footnotes.

Other Publications is a list of papers, articles and books written by Steve, some alone (like this one) and some in conjunction with others notably Peter Ainsley and Vince Golder.

Monday – Build Your Foundations

1. The Past Will Not Return

During our working lives we probably spend more waking time with our employer than we do with our friends and family; the organisation becomes an integral part of our lives. We know our workmates perhaps better than we know our relatives – their mannerisms, standard excuses, allowable weaknesses, when to trust and when not to trust.

Redundancy or unhappiness at work cuts off these relationships and leads to a sense of abandonment – however supportive family members and friends might be.

The bond between people and organisations can be so strong that I know of examples where a person's skills have been important to the organisation and, on leaving, a past colleague has called them back to sort out a problem.

Whilst the loyalty may be to the individual and not the organisation I have seen people go out of their way to resolve a problem for the organisation that has just dumped them – often to help out an old colleague where there is some residual personal relationships and a loyalty to one another.

However, please recognise that company loyalty is generally one-way only; how loyal has that organisation been to them? Why should they go out of their way to help an organisation that's just abandoned them?

There really was no need to return to sort out a problem of someone else's making.

The past will not return – accept the fact, let go as soon as possible, let the organisation sort its own problems.

And move on without looking over your shoulder.

Against this background it is hardly surprising that someone newly made redundant suffers disbelief that this could happen to them – they're losing a 'family'.

Panic can set in and turn the most rational of people into an emotional wreck so that logical thinking and sound decision making evaporate – and open the door for dejection and frustration to set in.

The situation can sometimes be made worse by others (not under the same pressure as you e.g. your partner) who might complain about your lack of progress! You will need to be quite resilient.

When under pressure the brain resorts to the 'fight or flight' reaction – it's an inherited survival mechanism. When under threat don't stop to work out what's happening, just run! Somehow, this ability to think under pressure needs to be re-established so you can begin to take a positive and thoughtful approach to your changed circumstances and not run from reality.

But <u>you are not alone</u>, this is happening to hundreds of people every day, so find a buddy or a group of people that will help to keep you positive, work hard to develop the right contacts with the right attitudes – they will benefit from you as much as you will benefit from them. And, as with the organisation, let go of those who depress you or hold you back.

There can be a lot of comfort in constructive mutual support which will re-energise your positive outlook when things are beginning to get a bit discouraging.

Look around at others in your section who may also be facing redundancy. Can you create a mutual self-help group to challenge and to support one another; later perhaps, in a new job working with past colleagues in a very supportive and professional relationship.

It is also good to seek out people who are highly successful in what they do because their attitude and enthusiasm will rub off – it's infectious.

The positive people you seek out don't have to have been successful in the workplace. Success can come from a variety of activities: coaching youngsters, playing a sport, gardening or faith groups – an environment where these people radiate the sort of enthusiasm and confidence you may need one day to get re-motivated when things are beginning to get you down.

Reprise 1 – Leave the past behind

What might drag you back into your old organisation? Past colleagues, a system you designed, the sports & social club.

List three possibilities:

1.

2.

3.

What will you do to ensure you don't get mired in the past?

Please be specific and perhaps look to networking opportunities or places of mutual (and positive) support.

_____

_____

_____

_____

_____

_____

_____

Having accepted that the past will not return, that the organisation that made you redundant is perfectly capable of looking after itself and you've now left behind those people who make a negative impact it's time to be a bit analytical and examine what it is that's making you feel tense and unhappy.

Obvious I know, but the drive behind all businesses is people and that people come in many different types. It's also worth reflecting that since Ancient Egyptian times the ones who get the privileges and status are rarely the ones who do the job – it's the administrators and politicians – those who look at how others have performed.

So, the chances are that you're in circumstances created by the people who have contributed little to the success or profitability of the organisation you've just left.

Understanding a little about these people can help put your current position into better context and help remove some of the self-doubt and uncertainty that comes with redundancy.

And that's where we go next.

2. Get Back That Old Confidence

The chances are that you have been beaten up for too many years by too many people who have got ahead of you through manoeuvring – not competence; and are better manipulators than you.

In my experience, such people maintain their position by a particular series of tactics, and if you're aware of these tactics and if you can take a dispassionate view of what probably happened to you you'll usually feel a lot better about yourself. These four main types of people include (3):

The **Control Freak** who starves the organisation of real information and might use instead testimonials, emotionally written and with a minimum of information; the alternative is to keep everybody subservient by the development of fear through spreading uncertainty.

The **Flooder** who provides too much information – often hiding contentious issues and might use glittering generalities along the lines of 'of course everybody knows...', or alternatively boarding the bandwagon of a noisy ginger group because 'this is what *everybody* wants'; when there is little evidence and even less substance.

The **Diverter** who readily changes direction to something easier or less politically sensitive and might use a technique called 'the transfer', answering a different question to the one posed, or calling in the uninformed to contribute – because this what the 'plain folks' want, again little evidence and less substance.

The **Muddier** who generates conflicting evidence to avoid a decision, or give the option to choose the decision of the moment; this individual might use loose words that can later be interpreted differently, or the soundbite to draw attention to the trivial and away from the important or contentious.

It's also worth noting that if a decision is going to be required these people will have lobbied the main influencers and senior management <u>before the critical meeting is held</u> to ensure any decisions taken are to their advantage – decisions that will normally be made by someone else to ensure they keep smelling of roses!

It helps to look back over these tactics to see where you might have been caught out; sometimes that knowledge will soften the blow because a degree of understanding often helps dispel some of the uncertainties that may have undermined your confidence or kept you attached to the organisation for much longer than is really necessary.

Many practical people – those who actually deliver the results the politicians depend on to keep their jobs – haven't got the patience to play silly games; games that are often played at the expense of the organisation.

Yet it's usually those practical people and those who have been made redundant who will bow to flattery and go back into the organisation that has let them down to resolve a problem not of their making (remember Section 1 – The Past Will Not Return). Don't do it.

A lack of planning on your part does not constitute an emergency on my part

Anon

Reprise 2 – Fighting back

Describe the type of person who hacks you off.

_____

_____

_____

How did (might) they manipulate you.

_____

_____

_____

What might you have done to deflect the blow?

_____

_____

_____

How will you build the resilience and confidence
to manage such people again?

_____

_____

_____

Having explored the characters whose sole interest is themselves and can be left to stew in a mess of their own making, you should now have regained a degree of self-confidence and energy. It's time to throw off the legacy of the old organisational culture and begin to look more closely at who you really are.

Much of our outward working character has been built up from a sense of duty, professionalism or the impact of those around us. Buried deep under those layers of armour is the person we would like to become again.

We must also acknowledge that the way we see ourselves is rarely the way others see us and many of us have a family that is a part of the conundrum, and should be involved not sidelined because 'I'm big and strong and can cope'.

The next section asks you to dig deep into what motivates you, using your experience of business and asks what you really want to do for yourself and family, and suggests you check the reality of your findings and assumptions with others.

3. Remind Yourself Who You Really Are

Spend some serious time to get to know yourself again and remember the good stuff that others may have suppressed so adroitly. Rediscover your accumulated expertise and those skills – many of which are transferrable.

A few of the questions you might ask yourself are:

What do I really enjoy doing? – meeting, creating, correcting, instructing – look back over your time at work, college or school and identify when and where you were at your most fulfilled, content and happy.

One method is to use a time line and plot how you felt (good and bad, add other emotions that matter) over the last years, a month at a time, when you were at your happiest what was happening at that time? What do you want to do more of and what do you want to leave behind?

What experience(s) do I have? – travel, competing, food & drink, religion – It's very easy to overlook your interests, for example a weekend hobby (cooking?) or understanding the culture of another country and to then ignore that experience on the basis that no-one else will be interested. Now is the opportunity to bring that interest to life, there will never be a better time.

What technical skills do I have? – by examination, by experience, by innovation – Is DIY important, are you a good mechanic? – A friend of mine built a sports car for fun, and he is an academic, no problem for him to side-step into an alternative type of job.

What aptitudes do I have? – being personable, hand/eye co-ordination, good memory - Can you move from an administrative job to one that demands dexterity or interpersonal skills for example. Can these aptitudes be developed and brought out in an alternative job?

What _didn't_ I like about my last job? – and be specific – company slow to respond, mind-numbing routine, too much going on – It's normal that over time the job content has changed, for example the bench scientist becomes an administrator pitching for government grants to keep the lab working – lots of discomfort and unfamiliarity; a series of changes that need to be recognised and addressed when looking at new opportunities.

What do I really want from a job (besides the money)? – challenge, advancement, power, security – Whilst there are a few people who are motivated solely by money, and will do whatever is necessary to get more of it; many people want to achieve and be part of the team

– so you need to identify the things that make a job worthwhile <u>for you</u>.

What has been my best position in an organisation? – do you want to continue fighting for position, or settle back into something less stressful and that you really enjoyed – Management pressures normally expect continual progression, where over-reaching can be as stressful as under-achievement.

What is the ideal level for you in an organisation, and how do you reach people at that level in a target organisation to check that it really is right for you?

What sort of organisation will be right for me? – Smokestack, PR, creative – There are distinct types of organisation and if you can identify those organisations that match your own personality the chances are that you will fit in easily, contribute readily and be an integral part of the team. See also Appendix 1.

What are my personal values (4)**?** – integrity, image, co-operation, informality, quality centred – Just as you will identify organisations that match your personality type, you need to consider the core values that are particularly important to you and to confirm through your own research that the values expressed by a target organisation relate closely to your own fundamental values and principles; if there's a significant mis-match then, no matter how good the money, the job will be miserable.

What do I want for my family? – Security, luxury, new experiences – At this time you will probably discover that the family is more important than you thought.

Your family can be very positive as a source of support and also, through a lack of understanding about your circumstance and level of anxiety, can also be an unknowing source of pressure!

What do my family want from my job (try asking)? – more time together, less time together, joint projects, less stress – When did you last make any long-term plans and what sort of job will meet these needs? The chances are you were too busy earning a living to have this discussion, and now that you're very busy looking for work you're still not having the discussion. Put time aside to find out – these are important people.

How do others see me? – it's good to get others involved: your partner, club buddies, children, past workmates – to ask them how they see you and to note their responses to the questions above – do they all give the same answers?

The chances are they won't all see you the same way and you will most likely come over to others as a different person to the one you see in the mirror each morning.

Where there is good agreement, excellent; where there is discrepancy it's because others see us differently to the images we have of ourselves. There may be little mannerisms to address, words that keep slipping into every other sentence, or just plain differences.

Don't try to justify how you appear or act – that's you; accept this to be the case and move forward unselfconsciously.

What did I actually do for a living? – we often lose sight of the bigger picture by being submerged in detail. Describe yourself and your last job to someone from outside your old work environment; this will help you get fluent in sharing your experience and expertise because you are bound to be asked what you've been doing or what you are good at – particularly during networking, or at interview.

One type of event I've found particularly useful for developing your 'presentation in an elevator (5)' is *Speed Networking*. You have less than a minute to describe who you are and what you're good at, and if any part of that presentation needs explaining you can modify it for the next person.

After five of six presentations you should find that you are quite crisp and clear and have developed your *Presentation in the Elevator* – 17 words that describe the benefits you can deliver in a way that will prompt a follow-on question when you can get into detail with someone who is now interested.

Later on, when developing your CV, you will find that this clarity is invaluable.

Reprise 3 – what turns you on

Be honest; you gain nothing by deceiving yourself.

Score from 1-9

What really turns you on at work?
- Power
- Influence   ____
- Recognition   ____
- Orderliness   ____
- Affiliation   ____
- Travel   ____
- Autonomy   ____
- Achievement   ____
- Challenge   ____
- Money   ____
- Security   ____
- Other 1_____ ____
- Other 2_____ ____

What really turns you on at home?
- Family   ____
- Property   ____
- Holidays   ____
- Culture   ____
- Friends   ____
- Hobbies   ____
- Other 1_____ ____
- Other 2_____ ____

How will you translate this information into the type of job you want?

Having identified inner drives and desires that are free from the baggage of a previous position and expectations, explored what is right for you and the family and had a reality check of ambition, appropriateness and personality it's time to examine where in industry you are likely to be at your most comfortable.

It is quite possible that when you first joined the organisation the department you entered was right for you but over the years with promotions and moves, as well as changes to senior management, the job changed subtly and relentlessly taking you with it.

Some work has been done with the character of organisations and attempts made to define this character with varying degrees of success (6).

The next section (along with appendix 1) asks you to look at your own character in a structured way and to try to match your real self and expectation with an organisation of a similar profile.

4. Find the Right Type of Organisation

You now know yourself, the confidence has returned and you know what you want to do in your next job. Now is the time to identify the type of organisation that's right for your particular skills and aptitudes.

Between entering and leaving an organisation, the chances are that the organisation will have changed (perhaps quite subtly) and for many years you have accepted whatever came your way as the 'organisational culture', however uncomfortable it might have become – but you will have retained your original personal values. There are many instances where these differences have resulted in significant strain and stress.

You are at one of the few times in life when you can stand back from day-to-day pressures and give serious thought to what is right for you, having been given this golden opportunity to start again with a new organisation and a lot less hassle.

In the main, organisations fall into ten categories (sorry to put them in boxes, but it's convenient) the ten types are described at Appendix 1 and are based on values derived from work done many years ago to explore personal drivers. So which of these ten types of organisation best suits your temperament and personality?

My recommendation is to use appendix 1 to pick two categories that are most appropriate to your own preferences and concentrate on these; this does not mean that if something worthwhile emerges from one of the other eight it should be ignored – go for it. At the very least it's valuable interview practice.

After some research and with experience you may find a different type of organisation is actually more suitable than the one you left, don't be afraid to lose the one that turns out to be inappropriate; replace it with something better. Selecting an inappropriate organisation will simply generate more stress down the line.

Armed with this knowledge you can start to go to market in a very positive way.

Reprise 4 – a bit more about you

There are a number of psychometric tests that should be used for an accurate assessment.

In the meantime this questionnaire will help you to focus your energies on the most appropriate type of organisation for you:

Please tick the boxes that best describe you

Things you like in a company	High	Med	Low	
Example: Socialising			✓	**Your type**
Technical stuff (research)				Calm
Constant change				Energetic
Being noticed				Extravert
Applied science				Introvert
Leisure centred business				Creative
Long-established & solid				Practical
Care and concern for others				Caring
Working to aggressive targets				Combative
Providing hospitality				Responsive
Sound detail and consistency				Organised
Strategy and planning				Calm
A charismatic leader				Energetic
Supporting other companies				Extravert
Systems and procedures				Introvert
Looking to the future				Creative
Safety conscious, sensible				Practical
Providing social support				Caring
Enjoying fast profit growth				Combative
Lots of travel & adventure				Responsive
A part of the establishment				Organised

Take those characteristics where you have scored *high*, compare them to *your type* in the right-hand column and see what type of organisation is most appropriate for you; then compare your result with the descriptions in Appendix 1.

Calm	Energetic
Extravert	Introvert
Creative	Practical
Caring	Combative
Responsive	Organised

If more than two types of organisation are appropriate, have a look in the 'low' scores and discount those that are opposite to your preferences.

Alternatively you can select the two that appeal to you most and omit the questionnaire completely.

Feel free to re-analyse your questionnaire in any way you see fit, this is just one possible approach.

Having identified two types of organisation that should be right for you with examples of each, it's time to explore and identify what drives that type of organisation and how its stakeholders are managed.

As you probe deeper it's possible that what seemed like a good idea turns out to be not so good – no problem, let go, revise your criteria and start again.

An organisation survives and thrives by providing its key stakeholders with benefits which can be tangible (money saved) or intangible (brand value – Harrods or Nike); it's now that you need to develop what you can bring to the table to help your group of target organisations serve their stakeholder(s) better.

The next section (along with appendix 2) looks at what appropriate benefits you can deliver into that target group and, along with the personal material from chapter 3, will provide the raw material needed to develop a convincing CV.

Tuesday – Get to Know Yourself

5. Package Yourself for Market

This is the time for a change in mind-set; so far you have been seeing yourself as a person, now you need to be re-packaged as a desirable and saleable commodity by adding some tangible deliverables.

When you buy a commodity (product or service), the most likely thing to influence your purchase is whether you actually like it; but when asked to justify why you bought it the reasons will most likely be practical: long lasting, wears well or its re-sale value.

For example, there are many cars that are sensible, cheap and economical so their purchase is easily justified on practical grounds. But they don't sell – why? Could it be because they don't appeal enough to the senses and emotions (of the middle aged boy racer?)

Think about the people you socialise with. It's not because they're particularly clever or skilful – it's because you like being with them. The same logic applies with hiring a person and despite bearing down on ageism, sexism, race or creed we still hire people because we like them and think they will fit well with the group, team or department.

The crucial change in mind-set is to change focus from what you want or need to one of being quite clear about what a prospective employer wants or needs – in the extreme case, the employer has no interest in you, just what you can do to enhance reputation or improve profit (or retained earnings).

Simply put, the employer is looking for the benefits that you can deliver. Benefits are divided into intangible benefits (what sort of pressure you can remove from your prospective employer's own job) and tangible benefits (what you can deliver in terms of quantifiable value). These are summarised in Appendix 2.

One intangible is your own personality which is likely to be pretty well fixed; it is important for the prospective employer to understand you because a mis-matched personality is very difficult to address, and if there is a mis-match between you and the organisation life can get pretty stressful for you both. Tangible benefits (many based on skills or expertise) such as technical ability that can be trained, and are relatively easy to address later.

Most organisations will need to justify interviewing you with technical or practical reasons. Commercial organisations exist to make a profit so at first interview you have to be able to show them where you can help improve the bottom line, it's usual that at the second meeting the interviewer will want to get to know you more as a person.

Tangible, deliverable, quantifiable benefits are important at senior level because in some of the major corporations there is a grading panel that assesses one's monetary value to the company; these panels tend to favour sales and marketing people because of the immediate value that these disciplines can often bring to the table. Similar panels can exist for less senior posts.

To get people to think about buying you, you need a sales brochure – that's your CV; a document that describes the package known as you; there is no set format (although agencies tend to have a 'house style') so surf, read and talk until you find a layout you are comfortable with, unless the prospective employer asks for a specific format.

The purpose of your CV is to take you to market by introducing you as a person and by describing and defining the tangible and relevant benefits you can deliver as a commodity.

The prospective employer needs to be able to justify to themselves and others why you should be hired, which they will do by your demonstrating an ability to deliver tangible benefits.

Reprise 5 – Your values

Score your personal values against those you perceive in the organisation you're applying to:

You – X
The organisation – Y
In common agreement – O

Define your goodness of fit to the target organisation								
Impulsive								Rational
Tough								Sensitive
Expecting								Thanking
Systems driven								People driven
Outcomes								Image
Loyal to self								Loyal to others
Competitive								Co-operative
Hierarchical								Informal
Low trust								High Trust
Closed								Open
Expediency								Quality
Traditional								Innovative
Do Now								Do later
Opportunistic								Developmental
Tactical								Strategic

Which are the biggest gaps?
Can you live with these differences?

Through the last three chapters you will have identified your personal desires and drivers, used these to characterise an appropriate sector of commerce or service that's right for you and researched that sector to be quite clear about the benefits they create and deliver to satisfy their key stakeholders' tangible and intangible needs.

This is an iterative process and just as you learn more about the particular sectors, so you will learn more about what they provide and how they provide it, so keep the information current and don't be afraid to revise it.

This short book is about taking yourself to market and any organisation or individual needs some form of credentials to attract buyers as well as to describe the benefits that will be delivered and how the purchaser will enjoy the product or service that delivers those benefits.

The next section builds on the previous three chapters to create your personal 'sales brochure' – your CV, and just as companies develop and enhance their products so can your CV be revisited and developed in the light of your experience and learning.

6. Building Your CV

(There is no perfect CV, so don't get hung up – but do look for examples e.g. on line)

In the first round of evaluating people for a job, a professional recruiter will give a CV about 12 seconds in which to assess a candidate for the post (7), and at this stage is probably looking for negatives – reasons to reject, not reasons to hire, the positive stuff comes later.

Mechanical scanning may be used where specific positive and negative words are searched, so please research the job and the company providing it and reflect the words from the job ad, or at least their sentiment.

There needs to be a section about you as a person. As well as your own assessment do take on board what your friends and family had to say about you when you were asking their opinion (re-visit Section 3 – Remind Yourself Who You Really Are).

This needs to be prominent for the recruiter to readily determine if you might be a good fit with the culture of the recruiting organisation.

If you wouldn't be right for the organisation and get rejected at this stage it may save you months of misery and tension trying to fit in to somewhere that's not right for you (8). If you're not right for the organisation, walk away – but that's much easier said than done!

Whilst people will interview someone because they might like them, the chances are that later they will have to justify the hiring on practical grounds which reflect the tangible benefits noted earlier and need to be included in the CV.

Many CVs I have seen describe just features, for example:

- in charge of a big budget,
- had so many direct reports
- profit responsible

None of which describes a tangible benefit (justification to hire) to the intending employer or to their critical colleagues and put simply are no more than features during your journey through various organisations.

One example of turning a feature into a benefit

When working with a major multinational, one of the people I worked with was a Progress Chaser who said she had nothing to offer; when we dug a bit deeper she had brought forward supplier delivery times from six weeks to two weeks on a £12m annual spend, this was worth £1m less tied up in inventory this year and every year.

In those days interest was about 10%. A simple calculation showed she had delivered £100,000 of working capital year on year (and this was just one of the tangible benefits we uncovered).

The Progress Chaser had not recognised the significance of this achievement herself and importantly it not been recognised by her management; yet here is something very desirable that was later included as a tangible benefit to help an organisation justify hiring her.

She went on to get a new job that was better paid and with better conditions.

How many of your own achievements do you take for granted or just gloss over?

Appendix 2 provides a structure to help define benefits; it's in two parts:

• <u>Intangible benefits</u> are what you can bring as a personality to a potential new organisation and the person hiring you; these will inform a selector of your likelihood to fit in well with the team and make a positive contribution without undermining the hirer's position or authority.

• <u>Tangible benefits</u> demonstrate that you have improved an organisation's commercial position and the personal standing of its management; things that provide the necessary business justification to hire you.

It's worth taking time to revisit and reflect on Appendix 2 from time to time as you work through the rest of this book.

Appendix 3 provides one style and layout for a CV.

Appendix 4 offers a very different style and layout for a CV.

Reprise 6 – More things to consider

Things you might easily overlook

Many of us have skills and experiences that we take for granted yet may be relevant to an employer, for example relatives overseas where you will have significant cultural skills.

List three such advantages here:

_____

_____

_____

Things you might easily overdo

It is very easy to get a bit carried away with things we're good at, or that we think could make an impression such as golf handicap, tennis or horse-riding (all require significant time – time often away from work) or unusual hobbies that are irrelevant or time-wasting.

List three such things to avoid:

_____

_____

_____

Having developed a CV that describes your tangible and intangible benefits in a way that is attractive to a specific group of potential employers it's time to give thought to how to identify suitable opportunities and appropriate target organisations.

The good opportunities are often unadvertised and come through people we know, yet these people may be unaware of what we can offer since generally, in the UK, we are reluctant to boast about our skills, capabilities and ambitions.

Dust off the soapbox and communicate more, because in these instances there is less competition for the post and by being referred you have a better chance of landing the position.

The advertised opportunities are open to all, and consequently the competition is much stronger, so your application has to be spot-on.

The next section examines ways to identify opportunities, some of the benefits and some of the pitfalls.

You should be prepared to change and amend your approach as experience and learning develops.

Wednesday – Get to Know Your Target

7. Reaching Target Organisations

There are a number of ways to get in front of potential employers, some more appropriate than others depending on the market, type of company and job requirements. Here is a selection; please see Appendix 5 for additional ideas and ways to stretch and develop this list.

The Direct Approach – Research the organisation, make sure you get the contact's name and title right; you know from experience that if someone spells your name wrongly it's an irritation and a turn-off; likewise if someone has worked hard for a degree, an award or a title it helps if this effort is correctly recognised in something as simple as the salutation on a letter.

Often the best person to aim for is the Managing Director because this position is aware of impending changes and (unlike most personnel departments) is not trying to fill gaps but looking to skills and aptitudes to move the organisation forward.

Response to a Job Advert – During our careers we have probably covered a number of functions and can create a CV and introductory letter for several different positions.

It is right to research the organisation before responding in order to pick up on values, culture, rate of growth, senior people, or customers for example; – is there any common ground you can exploit: particular customers or particular geographical outlets which demand a specific approach, contacts, particular expertise or a preferred means of communication.

Networking – Don't directly ask friends and colleagues for a job; ask if they know someone recruiting for your talents, if they know of an organisation that will be recruiting, or an organisation that is actively investing in new products, markets or equipment – all are opportunities.

If you can, it's good to get your colleague's agreement to use their name in your approach which strengthens your position (and is also a bit safer for the recruiter because they feel they can always blame someone else if things don't work out!) Consider joining appropriate MeetUp groups, Chambers of Commerce, Institutes or Learned Societies for example.

On-line – There are a multitude of job sites, some better than others; it's comforting to spend all day browsing thinking you're working hard – but often little happens. Use these sites by all means but do ration your time on them.

Remember the fight or flight reflex – for some people their situation can generate the flight reflex: getting somewhere safe and not straying outside the safety zone to meet people face to face (very stressful). These websites may also post imaginary jobs to get names on their books, or to appear more important than they really are in order to attract new customers to their services.

Social Media – Despite what some people might say, there is increasing mileage in using social media, if only because bosses talk to one another and might discuss the job you're looking for.

Additionally, someone endorsing you or talking well about you gives credibility when used with other approaches – just as traditional advertising had been used for years to give the edge over the competition.

Referrals – Something like 60% of decisions to purchase will be the result of a referral (9). Use social media and contacts constructively to ensure potential employers know you exist, that you are good to know and you are totally competent in what you do. These referrals may be from societies and institutes as well as directly from individuals. Later, these contacts may need you as much as you need them now.

Recruiters – Usually specialise in a particular field and are expert at reading a CV and matching people to companies and particular jobs. Meet a number of recruiters, narrow them down to three or four, get to know the individuals responsible for your sector – and then pester the hell out of them.

They may even help you develop your CV, and provide expert advice for free (if only to get you off their backs). The very least you should achieve is interview practice – even if the company you're put in front of isn't exactly right for you. This practice will be invaluable when you get the opportunity that really matters.

Your Own Contacts – I've already mentioned them several times, work them hard because one day they may need help from you – and if they're not prepared to support you now, do you want them to be with you in the future?

The Gentle Nudge – It's also good policy to regularly update your LinkedIn profile because the update is seen by your selected links and reminds them about you in a way that won't be seen as being 'pushy' – remember, you're working your contacts hard (even subtly at times).

Going Forwards

Treat your future as a project, with all the functionality of a project:

- Identify the resources you'll need and where to find them
- Find good sources of intelligence
- Read the adverts and opportunities critically
- Tailor your CV to the specific position
- Balance and integrate the different approaches
- Put time scales against activities (e.g. when to follow up)
- Put a clear structure to the campaign
- Find the support to maintain focus and momentum

Reprise 7 – Focus effort

Note the top two opportunities from each of the categories described below:

Target companies

1

2

Publications with job adverts

1

2

Networking groups

1

2

On-line sites

1

2

Social media

1

2

People who can refer you

1 _____

2 _____

Recruiters

1 _____

2 _____

Your own contacts

1 _____

2 _____

Profiles to keep current

1 _____

2 _____

It's a good idea to re-visit and refresh this list from time to time as experience grows.

Having identified two types of organisation that should be right for you and examples of each, the benefits they deliver and worked out how best to approach them it's time to get in front of the most appropriate people who will help you move forward.

As noted elsewhere, organisations have evolved to deliver ever more sophisticated products and services to stakeholders as needs and expectations change. An astute Board of Directors will be preparing for likely change and will need additional capable people to be part of that change.

But, those involved in personnel or recruitment generally respond to a demand or a brief from top management, they rarely create the demand themselves so the chances are that they are unaware of the likely future requirements of the organisation.

The key is to get yourself in front of that top management who may see a need coming and, whilst not hiring immediately, will keep your details handy. The next section develops this approach to give you the edge over others competing for the same post.

8. Go to Market – Aim High

One of the first jobs is to get your on-line profiles up to date; many people automatically check up on you here before responding to anything.

Aim high – pitch to the Managing Director (or equivalent) who knows which posts will be coming up in the future as the organisation expands, develops or changes shape. There may not be an immediate vacancy but in showing some initiative by addressing likely future needs your details may be kept on file – if only to save the cost of a recruitment campaign!

Many Personnel Departments will often be instructed to recruit <u>after</u> a change or restructure, so if your details are already on hand you may well have a head start. However, the Managing Director is probably the one orchestrating the restructure and could even put your details into the system in readiness.

Look also at adverts and news releases; not just jobs – if there's churn, there's opportunity.

In all cases study the advert very closely, refer back to the industry sector and consider the job requirements. If you've read the advert thoroughly there are lots of clues in it, even the way it's written and the use of grammar; then structure your approach *specifically* to that opportunity.

In most cases a generic response will simply be binned because it shows a lack of interest to the recruiter – the message it sends is that you can't be bothered to make the effort to land an opportunity that will change your life.

Lots of people claim to have sent hundreds of applications to no effect – this is often why!

Put a covering letter with the CV which is short and to the point with two main paragraphs, one about you as a person and one about the tangible benefits you delivered to your last organisation or the organisation you're still with.

And always finish with a positive close and ways in which this prospective employer can reach you, or close with a line such as *"with your permission, I'll give you a call in a couple of days to confirm you've received my application"* – you've just given yourself permission to follow up.

Reprise 8 – Write a letter

Yes – that's right, sit down with pen and paper to construct a letter to a possible recruiter.

By now you will have identified the ideal type of company, know what you can offer and what keeps you interested in the job.

Imagine someone you know as the hirer – for example from the golf club, social club or special interest group; the sort of person you would expect to find in your ideal company so you now know what will get their interest.

Understanding the recipient will help to structure your letter.

Remember – *The quality of communication is determined by the recipient.*

Here are a few ideas – please add your own.

Company Address   Your Address

If there a reference number use it

The date

A headline – that gets attention and is to the point

Dear (get the title right) (spell the name right)

1st paragraph, Introduce yourself and why you're writing

2nd paragraph, Important stuff – what you can offer (benefits)
 - Busy person, short and snappy
 - Someone with gaps in the day (e.g. publican) good flowing prose

3rd paragraph, Close with a reason to want to work with the company (huge respect, great products, flattery) and a call to action – what you will do next, for example 'with your permission I will call you before Wednesday to confirm receipt of this letter' – don't push too hard.

Yours sincerely (if you know them)
Yours faithfully (if you don't)

Signature

Your preferred contact details

Now ask someone else to read the letter and comment. Ignore the nice stuff from friends, because that's OK; and respond to the negative stuff which will improve your communication.

And don't get precious, the people you ask will be trying to help you, not put you down.

Having approached an organisation by addressing specific needs with a personality profile that matches the industry sector there will come a time when you're invited to be interviewed for an available post. **This experience can change your life.**

The euphoria of an interview has a similar effect to the despondency of redundancy – we forget all the effort and material that went into getting that interview, we don't plan and can appear out of our depth when we really need to show control and competence.

A professional interviewer will have spent quite some time preparing to meet you; these are busy people who value their time so if you make sure their time with you is well spent you will have the advantage over the less well prepared candidate.

The next section explores how to make the most of the short time you will have in front of the interviewer.

Thursday – Engage

9. Meet the Interviewer

<u>A note about people types</u>:

As a sweeping generalisation people tend to be warm or cold towards others; they may also be divided further into dominant and submissive types.

The four main types are:

Cold dominant people tend to have Spartan offices, want short pointed answers and don't allow you to correct mistakes – so don't make mistakes and be sure to know your stuff. They tend to make quick decisions and stand by that decision.

Beware the politician who sits in this box and pretends to be the warm dominant.

Warm dominant people have pictures on the walls, are quite focused, will accept a limited amount of 'lead-up' to a question and allow a couple of mistakes – provided these mistakes are corrected promptly; generally good leaders because they see things from perspectives other than their own.

In the main, deal with dominant people wherever possible – they actually make decisions.

Two other characters to consider are:

Warm submissive people are those who can chat all day and leave you with a nice warm feeling but with no decision or direction; in days gone by this used to be the bank manager – a secure job, not much pressure and a pillar of society.

If you were short of interview practice this was a good person to arrange a meeting with.

Cold submissive people are consummate analysts, every meeting will be scored against some sort of scale, and there will be no way to develop any sort of a relationship with this character – however hard you try.

The general rule is don't take 'no' as an answer from any of them except the analyst.

Don't be downhearted by the lack of progress if you're saddled with submissive characters, try to manufacture a second interview with a decision-maker when you can better demonstrate an ability to lead and persuade; but be careful not to be pushy, arrogant or rude.

Dominant Will make a decision		
The Politician Doesn't allow any mistakes	**The Leader** Allows a couple of mistakes	
The Analyst Works only with facts, impossible to build a relationship	**The Woffler** Will chat all day and leave you feeling nice and warm	
Submissive Will ask permission to make a decision		

Cold ... Warm

A note about the Analyst

This is the box (hate that term) that people migrate to when under extreme pressure – it's safer to work with facts than it is with people; whatever your inclination, be gentle – it may pay off later when the individual gets over the pressure and reasserts themself.

Reprise 9 – Answer the question

Imagine you have been asked "Tell me a little about yourself"

Should each type be answered differently?

For example:

Do you respond to the cold dominant with short and to-the point comments or the woffler with details about your last camping trip?

Jot down how you might respond to the different types of interviewer within 1½ minutes; give thought to content provided and ensure you provide the interviewer with something they would consider worthwhile to the company.

The Woffler (warm submissive)

_____

_____

_____

_____

The Analyst (cold submissive)

_____

_____

_____

_____

The Leader (warm dominant)

_____

_____

_____

_____

The Unemotional (cold dominant)
NB. – the politician is here but appears warm!

_____

_____

_____

_____

You now have a feel for the right sort of company, a CV that balances your capabilities and personality, a letter to send and some thoughts and ideas for the first interview.

There's a lot to hold on to and it may well be worth looking back over the notes so far to make sure that everything hangs together properly and that you haven't overlooked, or ignored, anything obvious (often the one thing that will let you down).

Everything you have created is from known material, critical feedback or personal experience, now is the time to enter unknown territory.

The letter and CV have got you through the door, once through that door there are a whole new set of rules and now, as well as verifying your CV, you have to get alongside the interviewer and begin to look ahead at how you can help the organisation move forward.

So far you have imagined an interviewer (or several) but haven't yet met one, so now is the time to prepare to impress and also to learn; because if this interview isn't successful you will gain a lot of experience to take to your next one.

10. Presentation and Follow-up

Many people have forgotten what it's like to be on the interviewee's side of the desk, so here are a few basic reminders to help provide some focus and examples of questions and tactics that can be used to give you a bit of extra confidence when meeting new contacts, putting yourself about and, importantly, at interview:

Respect the receptionist **as well** as the interviewer

Some companies will actually instruct their front desk to assess you whilst you wait to be called to interview. If you're off-hand, rude or aggressive you could have lost the job before you've even had the opportunity to meet the interviewer to present yourself.

In the interview it's possible you may be faced with someone awful, such as a bombast or an obnoxious youngster; whatever you do don't display your feelings – this could actually be a test!

Alternatively, you might be facing the sharpest mind that graduated last year, or a relative of the Managing Director.

This individual is your gateway back into work. Even if you're squirming stay nice and be alert.

Check the public face of the organisation

You should always check the company website to provide material about the company that will prepare you for likely questions and provide potential questions to ask the interviewer.

However, what goes into the website is what the company wants to show as its public face and you need to get under the skin so have a look at the more general questions below.

Another opportunity to prepare, if you know the interviewer's name, is to check out the individual in LinkedIn, it's possible you have common interests or hobbies that can be used to break the ice – you might also have rival football teams!

The four 15s

Something I learned a long time ago to help focus on the way into an interview – it's also useful in a sales situation with a new prospect when you're wanting to make a good first impression:

• The interviewer will form a tentative opinion from your looks and body language when you're about 15 feet away (don't forget clean shoes, including heels, especially if the interviewer is a woman).

• That tentative opinion will (usually) be strengthened closer up by your top 15 inches – head, neck, shoulders.

• The strengthened opinion will be confirmed within 15 seconds of starting the interview by how you talk and how well you relate to the interviewer.

• And then if you get it all wrong, it will normally take about 15 minutes to unconfirm that opinion and get things back on side.

You will probably form an opinion of the interviewer in similar fashion and if it gets to you, you've lost before you start; so please be aware that we have evolved to be suspicious of strangers and here you need to treat someone you don't know as a trusted ally (whether they are or not); and remember your boss-to-be might well be someone else.

Thoughts about communication

Communication comes in three flavours:

Body language – gives about **60%** of the message

Timing and intonation – gives about **30%** of the message

Actual substance – gives only about ***10%*** of the message – just listen closely to any political speech (10)

There's lots of material about the ***60%*** body language, much of it negative:
- Don't spread out your arms and legs, don't appear to dominate, and don't be withdrawn and timid
- Don't cross your arms and be defensive
- Don't scratch your nose, tug your ear or blink too much – looks as if you're lying or uncomfortable
- Don't glance to your right before answering the question – you're probably making up a suitably ingratiating answer

But do lean gently forward, be interested without being aggressive.

The ***10%*** of substance will be included in the CV and developed further during your interviews.

The remaining ***30%*** - ***timing*** and ***intonation*** is generally less well developed than body language or skills, although there are good books and related articles, for example about positive listening.

Timing: A key skill is to match your pace of response to the pace of the interviewer's delivery – too fast and you're over anxious, too slow and you're lazy. Listen hard to the interviewer – give them some space (11).

Giving the interviewer some space is not easy when under the many different pressures of interview. The secret is to respond not just to the content of the questions but to pick up on how those questions are delivered.

One client of mine managed to get it wrong on both counts – cutting across me in his enthusiasm to respond and leaving big gaps whilst digesting my response; I would have found this individual very difficult to work with if this is his normal self.

Intonation: Something I personally find very difficult especially when under pressure and trying to compose a sensible response.

One trap to beware is to speak carefully as you think hard to get the right sequence of events or explain a technical point – it can come over like a robotic response, which suggests you know the theory – but have you actually done the job?

Popular Opening Questions

These questions can be really useful in helping you settle into the interview and good interviewers will use openings like these to ease you into the conversation:

Tell me a little about yourself – personality, non-work activities and achievements. Don't be boring, clever or technical; two minutes maximum.

Why do you want this job? – the money of course, but encapsulate it within: challenge, the opportunity to make a difference, impressed with what the organisation is doing and that you want to be a part of it.

What are you most proud of? – only you can answer this, it's often good to have a response that's personal (climbed Everest) as well as a response that's business focused (opened the market in China, now worth £20m).

Tell me about your weaknesses – you can be a bit creative for some organisations, but try to find a way to make them positive – an old friend of mine used to fill in his self-appraisal forms with comments like: Strengths: single mindedness, Weaknesses: stubbornness.

There's nearly always a way to make things positive (just watch how the politicians perform).

Interview Closing Questions

Often we forget there will be the opportunity to ask questions at the close of the interview and it's easy to stumble here with some quite banal offerings:

• Does the canteen open late on Thursday?
• Where are the clothes shops?
• Do I need a code to work the photocopier?

We ask questions like these in order to fill the silence when later, on reflection, we wish we'd not asked anything.

This is actually a great time to demonstrate interest, the research you've done and that you're ambitious.

It is also a good opportunity to leave a positive impression on the interviewer.

People often remember most vividly the more recent events (including the conclusion of an interview), so take the time to be properly fluent in how you close the meeting.

Closing questions can give some good insights and demonstrate you've actually thought about the position and can also sharpen your presentation for the second or third interview.

Here are four closing questions that are generally considered to work well – both in demonstrating interest and also providing a second opportunity to remind the interviewer of you capabilities:

Are there any other candidates for this job?

- You can find out about internal candidates as well as external candidates, possibly even where you are in the pecking order and the likely time scale for a decision. It will also be a bit worrying if no-one else has applied.

What is it that made you want to interview me?

- A question that will help understand the values of an organisation and whether they match yours; it will give the priorities of the job which may be different to your expectations and, at the very least, it will strengthen your CV for your next interview if you don't get this position.

Which parts of the job are most important to the organisation?

- A question that should give an opening to the strategy of the organisation – where it's headed so that you can decide if you want to take the same journey, you can also remind the interviewer of the benefits you can deliver.

How would you describe your typical senior manager?

- A question that confirms you're ambitious and at the same time digging out expectations of long hours, travel, autonomy and what might be expected of you once you've joined and got over the selection people treating you nicely. It also elicits the degree of professionalism expected (and sometimes even an opportunity to turn the job down).

Three More Questions You Might Consider

What more would you like your customers to say about your organisation and its products?
 - An opportunity to add some specific beneficial skills and experiences appropriate to the post offered (in my own case it landed a different, and better, job than the one advertised).

What are the benefits your customers get from using the products/services your organisation sells?
 - Find out more about the customer focus and how sustainable the organisation is likely to be; without customers there's no cash flow to service the investors.

How would you describe the ethics of your organisation?
 - Perhaps more revealing will be the flannel and hesitations from a poorly managed organisation or from one that communicates badly.

If the tone of the meeting feels right you might also ask the interviewer what they thought of your CV and how they would develop it – it gives you a third chance to bring out the good bits and go back to the points you missed earlier. Take care that this doesn't offer a defeatist attitude, or signals that that you're looking for free advice to land a different job.

The follow-up – It's important

After the meeting it's often a good idea to send a letter to the interviewer thanking them for their time, sensitively remind them why you're the strongest candidate and use this opportunity to add any relevant bits and pieces not in the CV you provided or that should have been said at interview.

The temptation is to send an e-mail. An e-mail is easily deleted or put to one side for later; it's rarely read properly unless it's from the boss (or the bank!).

Much more interesting is to get something on paper that has to be opened (and yes, I know it's old-fashioned) but it will be remembered.

If you decide to send a letter, please use really good quality paper that would break your heart if you had to throw it in the bin; give consideration to layout and use language and grammar that reflects that of the interviewer.

And keep it short and to the point

Remember: Spell the recipient's name correctly and if the recipient has a title, award or big qualification (e.g. professor), then be sure to use it.

If you're unsure, ask the switchboard (it's easy) or use the website.

Referees

When you find you're close to getting the job the interviewer will probably ask for referees. For your referees to be able to answer questions about you in the most appropriate manner make sure they are aware of the job you're going for as well as your weaknesses and strengths (no-one's perfect) – send them a CV, brief them before you go to interview because they may be approached during the interview. Be sure to phone them after to keep them aware of how things are progressing.

It's also worth remembering that the best referee is the person you worked for immediately before applying for this post – so it helps if you didn't leave under a cloud.

Reprise 10 – Opening questions

Please write down how you would answer:

Tell me about yourself (see also Reprise 9)

_____

_____

_____

_____

_____

Why do you want this job?

_____

_____

_____

_____

_____

Tell me about your weaknesses

_____

_____

_____

_____

_____

It's also worth Googling 'Top Interview Questions' to widen the range and provide additional ammunition for the interview.

Here's some space for additional questions

Question 1

_____

_____

_____

_____

Question 2

_____

_____

_____

_____

Now look back over your answers and read them aloud – do they sound convincing? If not, go back over them again until they do.

There is an awful lot to get right at the face-to-face stage; the research, self-assessment and CV preparation are all considered activities that can be developed and refined with the luxury of time and reflection.

If you get a second interview, that's great – spend time in further research and preparation. However, it's possible that the first interview did not land the job or a second interview and you will feel knocked back a bit.

This is the time to reflect on the interview, how it went, the highs and the lows, where it went well and where you can improve. Some of the best sales people I know leave a call and whilst things are still fresh in their minds will complete a summary to identify where they can do better next time.

The next section provides a simple framework for such a summary which, in turn, provides a means to identify which areas you can build on to strengthen your presentation for the next interview.

Friday – Control and Some Alternatives

11. Build Resilience

Finding a job is a bruising process and it's very easy to get dispirited, especially when those receiving your application have never been out of work themselves, and so can't appreciate the pressures on someone seeking employment.

Not only should you build resilience, you should also learn from every communication, every meeting and every interview to develop a process of continual improvement.

It helps to keep a record of what happens, and where in the process it happened; below is an example of a range of headings that you can add to, remove, amend or modify as you find appropriate:

- Applications sent to MDs
  - Number of responses
  - % Success
- Applications to personnel
  - Number of responses
  - % Success
- Telephone conversations
  - Requests for more information
- First interviews, how you felt about:
  - Opening, meeting and greeting
  - Personal appearance, consistency with the interviewer?

- Interviewer type
  - Communication skills
  - Body language
  - Timing & intonation
  - Content
  - Opening questions
  - Closing questions
- Follow-up
- Second interviews

In some areas you'll find you're very strong e.g. letter-writing but others not so strong e.g. questioning skills. A scoring mechanism will allow you to identify which areas to work on and, if necessary, where to ask for help – all of which builds that resilience, leads to continual improvement and adds extra purpose to your job search.

Reprise 11 – Interview improvement

Letters, CVs and e-mails can be evaluated at leisure; the one area where emotion is immediate is during and after the interview.

Create a score sheet that can be used in the car park (or someone else's car park) immediately after the interview process. Section 10 provides a starting point.

For example

Score 1-5 (1 poor; 5 good) for how you felt the following elements went:

Element	Score	Remedy – if scored below 3
Reception		
15 Feet		
15 Seconds		
Empathy		
Continue with what's important to you		

After a number of interviews it's possible that you feel you can't improve some areas of your delivery, you're as good as you think you can be – yet you're still a bit unsure whether there is scope for improvement elsewhere.

The chances are that there is scope to improve, even the very top sportspeople have coaches despite being among the best in the world.

In analysing the summaries from a few interviews it should become clear which areas could benefit from some objective and constructive support.

This is addressed in Section 13

An option that might arise is a degree of confidence in that you can go it alone and there might be some benefit in being your own boss – if only for a short time until you land the right paid job.

The next section offers some thoughts on what might be the right self-employed option for you.

If you are persuaded that self-employment is definitely out, please skip the next section.

12. Going it Alone?

For some people the idea of going back into work, with the political pressures and deadlines to meet, no longer feels appealing and the opportunity to be your own boss begins to look increasingly attractive.

One approach is to examine your own preferred style of working – from total independence to being managed. No particular situation is any better than any other, it's what is right for you that matters.

There are many ways into self-employment, and some are more appropriate for you than others.

For example if you dislike conformity then franchising is unlikely to be right for you; many of the franchisees who are released from their contract get into that situation because they have added their own 'improvements' without the consent of the franchise owner.

Similarly if you are not the innovative type then the life of the entrepreneur is probably wrong for you. It is said that the entrepreneur looks at the same thing as you or I, sees something different, and then exploits that difference.

Opposite is a decision tree that goes through the major options to help reach an outcome that is right for you.

But it comes with a <u>Health Warning</u>. ***The aim is to cause you to think more deeply, not to provide a definitive answer – only you can do that.***

Decision Tree

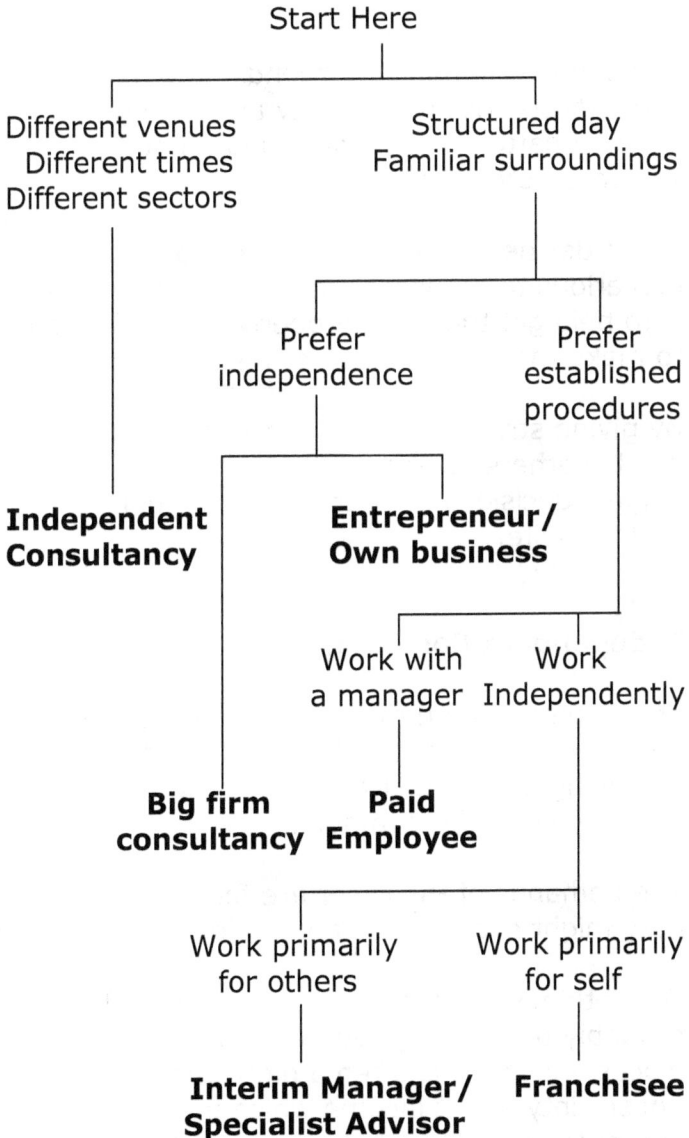

Start Here

Different venues
Different times
Different sectors

Structured day
Familiar surroundings

Prefer
independence

Prefer
established
procedures

**Independent
Consultancy**

**Entrepreneur/
Own business**

Work with
a manager

Work
Independently

**Big firm
consultancy**

**Paid
Employee**

Work primarily
for others

Work primarily
for self

**Interim Manager/
Specialist Advisor**

Franchisee

One theme that runs throughout self-employment is the impact the change might have on your family and friends. You may be comfortable with uncertainty and strange working patterns but others might find this extremely stressful.

The order below works from the most precarious to the least precarious and the idea is to help get thoughts properly marshalled and to make the decision clearer and more definite.

By giving structure to the process it is easier to involve others in what could be one of the biggest decisions of your life – and your partner's life.

Independent Consultancy

This is perhaps the most precarious option and demands a good general understanding as well as having a particular area of strength such as strategy or HR for example.

The demands of the client are far more than they might expect from an employee.

Other things to consider include: you will probably be working odd hours, perhaps in odd places and there is often a high level of uncertainty about income which might be alright for you, but what about your family?

Entrepreneur/Run Your Own Business

What is important is to clearly identify what will differentiate your operation from others in a similar field; in marketing terms your Unique Selling Proposition (USP) – but looked at from the standpoint of the customer and supported by a clear statement of the benefit(s) your product or service will deliver; a note about benefits is included in appendix 2.

This option will normally demand your own money or borrowed money which is secured against assets you own such as your house. This may be fine for you, but what about your family?

Specialist Advisor

The specialist advisor has built up a bank of specific experience and knowledge that needs to be widely broadcast to alert people to the fact that this capability, experience and expertise is available – often as a niche player.

To adopt this option you will need to be an excellent self-publicist or have a network of people who know what you can deliver as a specialist. Often a good early customer is the organisation you have just left, but without follow-on work there's a risk you will be left high and dry.

Interim Manager

The Interim Manager is exactly what it says on the tin, not a consultant, not an advisor, not a permanent employee but someone who fills a key role in an organisation for a defined length of time acting as a paid manager during that period.

The role may be to maintain a position until a new person can be appointed, for example a counterpart from a competitive organisation who is working out their six month contractual obligation, or to manage a one-off project such as closing a division or restructuring the financial reporting process.

Again, where will the next job come from?

Big Firm Consultant

This may be the position for someone from corporate life or the public sector where there are established ways of doing things, close relationships with key clients and support provided from a central function.

The work is often quite specialist in nature and might span the client's international operations e.g. the annual audit or may be highly specific and detailed such as devising a new IT infrastructure to meet a revised corporate strategy.

Franchisee

The benefit of a franchise is that the concept is tried and proven to work and is backed up by sales materials with the better franchises having genuine specialists available to advise and support.

To take this route it is worth remembering that a franchise generally works to the very rigid procedures and specifications that form the basis of the brand strength.

Many franchisees have had their franchise removed because they have embellished the core offering or adjusted it to suit local circumstances without clear permission to do so.

Normally buying a franchise will involve quite a significant outlay or level of borrowing which could be at risk if things don't work out.

As with other options, there is a need to consider the family and how they will react to the new situation.

Paid Employee

Perhaps reconsider the idea of self-employment?

Note – whatever your decision about self-employment, this book is primarily about finding a paid job and whilst many of the tools and techniques work well with self-employment, e.g. selling benefits, you are advised to seek additional competent advice before embarking on that particular journey.

It is recommended that the additional advice is initially by person to person contact. Websites and the like will only paint the ideal picture for an average business. Far better is an established advisor with broad business understanding who will save you significant time and money.

Reprise 12 –Is your choice really right?

Having decided which is the best course of self-employment there is great benefit in discussing this with people who know you well and who will challenge as well as support.

Please note your preferred option:

_____

Now define your market

_____

_____

_____

The key benefit you provide into that market

_____

_____

_____

And how you will you beat the competition

_____

_____

_____

Please note: competition is for the money spent, not just the quality of the goods or services you provide – so check for unlikely alternatives to your own offering.

Now find three good reasons why it can't work:

Reason1

_____

_____

_____

Reason2

_____

_____

_____

Reason3

_____

_____

_____

Now state clearly what you will do to overcome each of these reasons:

Remedy 1

_____

_____

_____

Remedy 2

_____

_____

_____

Remedy 3

_____

_____

_____

When you are content that you can overcome the objections (whether real or imaginary) you should have sufficient confidence to move forward.

There are a number of people setting themselves up as self-employed who have come from a corporate background, for example banks or the public sector and because of their history feel they are equipped to advise the small business or the job-seeker.

The reality is that corporate life is quite cushioned with experts to provide support, and ready access to information where required. It is a rare individual fresh from corporate life who has developed the breadth of understanding or depth of knowledge to advise appropriately.

Other points to consider include the global scale of information at corporate level when the self-employed person will normally be concerned with a relatively small and specialist geographical area. Often corporates have a tendency to underestimate the capability of someone looking for work or the acumen of the small business owner/manager.

We turn next to some opportunities for support that might be available to help you change your employment situation.

13. Support & a Note of Caution

One of the main things to recognise is that you have not been singled out and are isolated, others have been through this process before you and some are going through it now.

Help and support can come in a number of forms with varying degrees of helpfulness and include:

Others who have recently left a job and think they know how to manage someone else's circumstances (but may not).

Specialists who know what they're doing but can be quite expensive (and rightly so).

Facilitated self-help groups to provide guidance whilst you gain mutual benefit from others also looking for a new position.

Free help from institutes and government.

Some are outlined in more detail below

The Recently Redundant

Those who have recently been made redundant will be very varied e.g. personnel managers or bankers. Some have the feel, skill set and understanding to provide genuinely helpful advice; others will cheerfully take you for a ride to get their hands on some of the severance pay that you need more than they do.

If you decide to use the recently redundant, check their credentials thoroughly; even use the meeting with them as a practice interview to put yourself in the interviewer's shoes and gain a bit of insight into the process. Even take out references.

The Specialists

Even the specialists can be quite variable and as noted above with the Recently Redundant, you have the option to treat any meeting like an interview – with you in the chair.

And, if you are lucky enough to have a redundancy package **then you are in the driving seat** and <u>not the specialist</u> – however convincing they sound, use your position to advantage:

Probe, dig and use the old tactic of Y^2: every question has a follow-up question, for example:

- <u>Why</u> do you think you can help me? (experience)

- <u>Why</u> do you think that experience is appropriate to my specific skill set?

Use it on them, because later people will use it on you! And always remember they've had more practice than you, so learn by how they answer, or how they deflect or duck the question.

In my experience the specialists range from the highly ethical and professional to those organisations that seem to have been established to draw as much money from government as possible by providing 'training' – some of it of a quite dubious nature.

Facilitated Self-Help Groups

If a number of you are being made redundant at the same time e.g. the closure of a department or the relocation of a division then you can club together to meet at a regular time with a capable facilitator.

Develop a programme that works through the elements described in this book, setting principles and guidelines along the way. You will form into loose groups to explore who you are, where you're at your best, develop a CV and practice interviewing.

Your colleague(s) will challenge you and support you – as you will do for them, use the old dictum that the best way to learn is to teach. The facilitator will open the session, leave you to get on with it, and be on hand if there are queries or if clarification is required. You will also build strong contacts who may be able to lead you into an organisation if they get there first, or to act as suppliers or customers when you get into new employment.

The one key requirement to make this work well is a good facilitator who can ensure that ego, (past) position, (past) seniority, formality and politics are left outside the room.

Free Help

In addition to consultants and coaches clamouring for your money, there is actually a good deal of free help, especially if you belong to an institution or society; for example the Chartered Management Institute's website has a great deal of useful and appropriate material that its members can use to expand on the notes here; there is an Association of Interim Managers and various consultancy groups, all of whom can be helpful.

If you don't belong to an institution the local library is a good place to be because, in addition to the journals and papers, you will meet other people also seeking employment and others who can provide ideas and insights – possibly with industry or employer experience.

It's very easy to become isolated and insular whilst you feel miserable and unloved, but there are others on the same journey – go and cheer each other up, starting with those who have the most positive attitude.

Costs and Cautions

Friends and the Recently Redundant come free so there is no immediate cost, however their advice may be misplaced and you end up with a significant long-term cost (both financially and emotionally) if you find yourself in the wrong job or waste an inordinate amount of time chasing rainbows.

Specialists are expensive in the short-term but their long-term benefit can be significant if you end up in the position that's just right for you.

Facilitated Self-Help Groups are inexpensive in the short term because everyone chips in to spread the cost and beneficial in the long term because you should unearth the job that's right for you, and you will have made some useful contacts in the process.

Free help may be beneficial in the long term with valuable contacts from the library where, between you, you will have created an informal self-help group of supportive people who could stay with you for many years.

Be Choosey over who you work with. If necessary explore the idea of a cost/benefit analysis

And remember – It's you in the driving seat

Reprise 13 Identifying support

One option is to use the format of a risk analysis and score various parameters against your personal circumstances; for example if you have a big redundancy package a professional fee might be acceptable, if you're on income support it isn't.

Opposite is a part-constructed table to provide a template that you might use to assess what order of priority to give the different types of support:

1. Give each of your personal **factors** a weighting dependent on your circumstances, from 1 (not acceptable) to 5 (very acceptable). - For example you may have a big pay-off and score 4 for a professional fee being acceptable to you.

2. Then score each of the **supporter**'s factors from 1 (poor/unacceptable) to 5 (good/ideal) - For example someone who is out of work might score a 5 for availability.

Multiply together the personal weighting and supporter's score to give a figure for that factor; do the same for the other factors and you will have a series of totals where the highest total is the most likely to be the right advisor/supporter.

Factors / Support	Weighting	Recently out of work	R.O.W score	Specialists	Specialist scores	Self-help groups	Self-help score	Add more
Trust	5	3	**15**	4	**20**	2	**10**	
Cost	4	5	**20**	2	**8**	5	**20**	
Availability	1	5	**5**	4	**4**	5	**5**	
Add more options	A	B	**AxB**	C	**AxC**	D	**AxD**	
Totals								
Rec. out of work			**40**					
Specialist					**32**			
Self-help groups							**35**	
Additional Options								

In the scenario above, the recently unemployed are the best option and specialists the worst option.

Please create the risk assessment that's specific to your circumstances (Excel works well here).

14. In Conclusion

- You now know yourself
- You know what turns you on
- You have identified appropriate benefits that you can deliver
- You have a CV that works
- You have a plan of attack
- You have some good friends and contacts
- You are energised

So: Get Stuck In, Happy Hunting and Enjoy

- That's right, enjoy

Nil Illigitimi Carborundum
(Don't let the bastards grind you down)

Steve Mullins
April 2015

Weekend – Relax and Reflect

Appendices

Appendix 1 – Types of Organisation

Using the summary from *Reprise 4* you should readily identify where you ought to be comfortable working. Please note this is to provide a basis for ideas and should not be used as a definitive result.

Organisations can be divided into ten different types based on 'The Big Five' – a tool sometimes used to assess a candidate; the aim is to match your preferences to an organisation with similar characteristics.

Calm: a focus on technical matters or research and may include consultancy and strategic planning; examples might be Johnson & Johnson or Boots.

Energetic: dependant on a charismatic leader and readily embraces change; examples might include Virgin or the film industry.

Extravert: organisations that maintain a high profile and often work to develop or support other organisations; examples might include PR agencies or corporate sales.

Introvert: tend to focus on applied research and development, systems, procedures and controls; examples might include Bell Laboratories or established engineering companies.

Creative & Imaginative: centred around lifestyle and leisure and also embrace the future; examples might include theatre or fashion.

Practical & Conservative: organisations with a long history and a record as a 'safe pair of hands' thought of as 'sensible'; examples might include the utility companies.

Co-operative & Conflict Averse (Caring): involved very much with caring and social support; examples might include charities, hospitals or the police.

Combative & Competitive: always driving and being driven to meet aggressive targets, with a focus on fast profit growth; examples might include merchant banking or gaming software.

Responsive & Market Focused: include hospitality and events as well as travel and adventure; examples might include hotels or adventure holidays.

Organised & Disciplined: centred around detail and consistency or as part of the establishment; examples might include admin or the public sector.

Appendix 2 – Defining Benefits

Original research (revised in 1998) identified that in product marketing the reasons to buy things are a balance between delivered benefits (tangible) and perceived benefits (emotional).

And the ratio of influencing the decision to buy is about 30% delivered benefits to 70% perceived benefits.

i.e. today 70% of our decision to buy is based on <u>our impression </u>of the good or service.

However, when we are asked to justify the purchase our explanation is based on what it does – not that it appealed and we liked it, – how many people do you know who drive the cheapest car available and justify their vehicle on some sort of economic grounds?

I had this discussion with a client some years ago when asking him to justify an enormous Mercedes, the reasons were along the lines: starts first time, a good resale value, if I forget the service, it just keeps on going etc. etc – all practical justifications. When I said 'Rubbish – it's so you can park it in the drive to tell the neighbours you've made it, or draw up at the Savoy and have it parked' he nodded and agreed that those were indeed the real (intangible) reasons.

So, the CV needs to have a section about perceived benefits – what you as an individual can bring to the party for example as a team player, as well as a section that will justify your being hired e.g. the savings you made for your previous organisation during your career. This goes on the front page as a personal profile; details about hobbies can come later.

2.1 Perceived Benefits

The perceived benefits are similar whether directed to a manager, a team, or an organisation. They revolve around four phrases:

Reassurance – that my background and skills are right.
Confidence – that I can be left alone to get on with it.
Don't worry – I have done this before.
Peace of mind – that it will be done right, and on time.

And may be augmented with:

Leading edge thinking/experience/training
Mental stimulation for the organisation
A challenge to the status quo

I suggest these latter options should be used sparingly and only with organisations that have the drive, maturity and energy to accept criticism and rise to a challenge.

An option when they are included in the CV is to use them in retrospect: "I have the skills to ensure projects that were slipping got completed on time which gave colleagues and management the peace of mind to let me oversee other projects whilst they got on with their own work".

2.2 Delivered Benefits

2.2.1 – Benefits to the Organisation

Whatever the organisation, money plays a part:

- For the commercial organisation it's about growth, investment and dividends.

- For the charity or not-for-profit it's about being able to put more into the community.

- For the public sector it's (slowly getting to be) about saving costs and actually delivering value for money.

These financial targets can be summarised by:

- **Image** – relates to sales, the better the image of the organisation the higher the price or the greater the volume of sales, or both (relates to income in the Profit & Loss Account).

- **Finance** – how the money is used by the organisation to get best value for any expenditure (relates to Gross Margin in the Profit & Loss Account).

- **Performance** – getting a bit more from what already exists (relates to Overhead Management in the Profit & Loss Account).

The ways these targets may be approached is to:
• Save
• Solve
• Increase
• Improve
• Reduce or
• Remove
something that directly impacts upon one or more of the financial targets.

One example is noted earlier with the Progress Chaser, other examples may include:

• Opened new markets which increased sales by ww% (image).

• Reduced inventory to release working capital of £xx (finance).

• Sped up a process to increase capacity and so reduced the need for planned investment by £yy; this can apply to admin as well as to manufacture (performance).

All of these need to be quantified in financial terms, for example "reduced inventory by 5% on an annual spend of £20m thereby saving working capital to the value of about £1m per annum"; there needs to be a measurable outcome that demonstrates value to the company.

2.2.2 Benefits to the Decision-Maker

People have different drivers at work and if you can be seen as a means to develop the standing of your boss-to-be then you become desirable. A lot of caution is needed in how the benefit is worded; otherwise it can look like a bribe!

Different people have different drivers which are satisfied by benefits; experience suggests the more usual managerial drivers are:

• Power (Managing Director)
• Influence (Finance Director)
• Recognition (Sales & Marketing)
• Achievement (Research & Development)
• Orderliness (Administration)

Other drivers may address:
• Safety
• Affiliation
• Security
• Challenge
• Wealth
• Travel

The same approach is used for the decision-maker as the one used for the benefits to the organisation i.e. Save, Solve, Increase, Improve, Reduce, Remove – something or other that will impact on one or more of the personal drivers noted above.

Wording these benefits is difficult, because it can sound like some sort of inducement "hire me and I'll make you famous"; so perhaps something along the lines of "the project I managed saved £250k and was recognised across the company with an award formally presented to the Team Leader".

In addition to the positive benefits noted above there are also a number of concerns that you can play to by providing ways to take away, or massage, the particular concern:

• Ego – noted above under drivers

• Fear – may be caused by new legislation or a new piece of software; if you can demonstrate problem-solving capabilities in an environment that is unfamiliar to the boss, or demonstrate previous experience of that environment, you become desirable.

• Guilt – "everyone's got one, why haven't I?" If you can deliver one or explain why, you become desirable.

• Greed – do you have the skills or experience to help the boss abstract more of a personal nature (without compromising business and personal ethics) – if you do, you risk becoming desirable.

• Ignorance – what is the competition up to? If you can shed some light, you become desirable.

And finally, when you look at your draft CV and read a list of features:
• Managed a £25m budget
• Had 75 direct reports
• Responsible for five branch offices

Ask yourself the question ***"So What?"*** and keep asking "So What?" until you have drilled down to one of the benefits discussed above.

And please, split multiple features – for example "I managed a £25m budget with 75 direct reports" into separate and distinct statements, each with its own clearly articulated benefit (whether tangible or intangible).

Benefits Summarised

Perceived benefits

- Reassurance – a beer that's reassuringly expensive
- Confidence – a toothpaste's ring of confidence
- Peace of mind – that all is well
- Don't worry – I can deliver
- (and possibly) Leading edge – a challenge to accepted wisdom

Delivered benefits – to the organisation

- Save
- Solve
- Increase
- Improve
- Reduce
- Remove

Something or other that impacts on
- Image (turnover)
- Finance (gross margin)
- Performance (overheads)

Delivered benefits – to the decision-maker

- Power (MD)
- Influence (FD)
- Recognition (Sales & Marketing)
- Achievement (R&D)
- Orderliness (Admin)

<u>And playing to</u>:

- Fear
- Ego
- Guilt
- Greed
- Ignorance

And answers the question

"So What?"

Keep digging until you find the tangible benefits

Appendix 3 – One Layout for a CV

There is no perfect CV, so don't be afraid to create something that is right for you – but do check on-line sites such as Monster for ideas and different presentations.

Some of us are a bit ugly or touchy about our age so if you want to omit specific details then do so, there is also legal precedent for omitting those things that can be construed as a form of discrimination.

That said, it must be remembered that the CV is the first point of contact and at this stage the recruiter's aim is to get to a manageable pile of applications and is looking at reasons to reject – as is the electronic reader if one is being used; reasons for positive selection come later.

If it will help to omit details such as age and you feel it is right to do so then please go ahead, because once through the first trawl these aspects will find their way out at interview.

<u>But</u> the key objective is to get through the (de)selection process and to that first interview – it's not to create a literary work of art; it is to package yourself as a desirable purchase and to take you into a highly competitive market.

It should also be re-iterated that the CV should be specific to the post and not generic – a generic CV is quite obvious and will usually find its way directly into the bin.

Below is one format that has worked well for many people for many years.

It isn't necessary to get everything into one page but it is important to get the key points on the first page.

If the material is convincing enough and you move to the point of genuine selection the recruiter will normally take the trouble to read subsequent material thoroughly; so there is scope to provide several additional pages of job-relevant information.

Example page 1

CV for Steve Mullins	
Personal details	**More personal details**
Photo?	Status
Date of Birth	Phone
Address	E-mail
Education	**Qualifications**
University	Degrees
College	A-levels
School	GCSEs/SATs
Career summary	
Last Co. with dates	Position - Director
Prior Co. with dates	Position - Manager
Prior Co. etc.	
Personal profile	
Team player, self-starter, creative etc. The intangible benefits This can be a good place to put awards, for example, up front and in the selector's face.	

Example page 2 and subsequent pages

CV for Steve Mullins continued	
Employment history (most recent first)	
From date – to date	**Company 1** - name
Write a bit about the company; it's reach, it's products, turnover, number of employees. The interviewer may have heard of the organisation but not aware how impressive it is	
Job title	
What the job actually involved, job titles can be misleading e.g. *Development Manager* may be a creative scientist of a sales person – each demanding very different aptitudes and skills	
Responsibilities & achievements	
Responsibility, then tangible benefit	
Responsibility, then tangible benefit	
From date – to date	**Company 2** - name
A bit about the company	
Job title	
Etc.	
Continue with as many pages as necessary	
Hobbies and interests	
Not strictly necessary, but if you have done something particularly relevant or that you're proud of don't be afraid to flaunt it; Care with golf, horse-riding, junior football though – things that can take over from the job	

Appendix 4 – Another Layout for a CV
(IN THE MUSIC HALL TRADITION – I ACTUALLY GOT THIS PUBLISHED!)

STEVE MULLINS' CV - AS A MONOLOGUE
WITH APOLOGIES TO STANLEY HOLLOWAY AND MARRIOTT EDGAR
(WORKS WELL WITH A YORKSHIRE ACCENT)

There's a spot in many a company
That's often quite tricky to fill.
It's to exploit new ideas and new markets
With panache and grace - and some skill

So approaching the chap that looks after the staff
"I know a lad wi' a story to tell"
He said "Who?", I said "Me"; He said "Thee?", I said "Aye"
He sighed, he replied, "Bloody 'ell"

I got my degrees and I joined Express Foods,
Making butter and cheese to enthral
Then I went to Lane Ends with some marketing friends
Learned about brand share, Boston and all

Now as a marketing man, I was in deman...
...d to companies keen for a SWOT
Head hunted by Mars, I thought 'chocolate bars'
But ended up with the catering lot!

Seven years they flew by, till this director guy
Told me how to do something quite arty
I pointed out he knew nŏwt, and then he,…
with a shout
Said "get on thy bicycle smarty"

My next stop was cigs - having given them up!
With Gallahers – the job was a treat
I invented new things for pubs and for work
And brought them to market *tout suite*

But life in the corporate was becoming a bind
Where decisions were things to avoid
I'd been hired, retired, rotated and fired
It was time to become self-employed

Two decades have passed since I joined with a
firm
That, after schooling, it promised a resultant
To have new pals, new tricks and new things to
learn
And to earn – as a busy-ness consultant

I was caught, then taught, and after that
sought
Work in a de-clining mark-et
Life was quite bleak, with no money to speak
Of, a family, big mort-gage and debt

The Enterprise programme it came and it went
The 'Blue Whoosh' was a symbol of saviour
Much bacon it saved in a struggling trade
And did consultants a thumping great faviour

(Sorry)

I've helped firms with their planning, their selling, their manning
To achieve significant growth
There's big 'uns and small 'uns and some in between
Keen to sell more, put up prices – or both

The key to these wins has been to do different things
Put rules aside and look from anew
To break with tradition, some call it sedition
Like this CV – that's here – before you

The aim's to explain what's given me fame
It's to look at things in a new way
To provide an approach that's not been used before
And for an appropriate level of pay

So if any of your projects could do with a lift
And an approach that's both tailored and new
Please give me a call, I could do with the work
- And p'raps recognition for you.

--.—

For additional copies of this CV,
Or offers of substantial work,
Please contact:
Steve Mullins

Appendix 5 – Lead Generation

42 Sources of Leads
(Thanks to Vince Golder – MD of Goldnet Referral Marketing)

Please check for special terms, for example added costs, lock-in clauses, contract duration or other hidden extras.

This list isn't exhaustive, but should provide some thoughts and opportunities to get you and your capabilities in front of people who may hire you, remember you or refer you.

A much fuller list is available from Vince on Kindle with his articles about *Referral Marketing* and *Personal Presentation.*

<u>At no cost or at minimal cost</u>

01. Use of LinkedIn
02. Use of E-cademy
03. Canvassing business parks
04. Customer referrals
05. Workmate referrals
06. Ex-boss referrals
07. Testimonials
08. Develop and post an 'employee charter'
09. *Give-to-get* with contacts, allies, workmates and others
10. Volunteering

11. Publish a book
12. Publish a white paper
13. Reciprocal referrals
14. Referrals from the bank manager and other professionals
15. E-mail marketing (careful with spam)
16. Post a video to YouTube
17. Contribute to on-line forums
18. On-line searches
19. Visit shows, events, seminars etc.
20. Public speaking
21. Job ads – where there's churn there's opportunity outside the particular job ad.

At low cost

22. Alliances, joint venture partners
23. Endorsement strategy programme
24. Door to door calling
25. Press releases from you
26. Press releases about you
27. Reverse sell from any junk mail
28. Reverse sell from cold calls
29. Telemarketing to new prospects
30. Telemarketing to past contacts
31. Blogging
32. Develop a personal brand (include social media)
33. Agencies – should be low cost, or free, to join

At medium cost

34. Advertising in Local Directories
35. Advertising – Leads Incorporated
36. Direct mail (individual)
37. Direct mail packs (with others)
38. Join a sports club
39. Join an appropriate association
40. Marketing cards (like business cards but with more detail)
41. Referral cards (more detail than a marketing card)
42. Business networking

And please do follow-up on all initiatives – the follow-up itself can generate interest and opportunity.

Appendix 6 – A Bit Deep & Meaningful

*It's SMART, but is it is a Commercial Objective,
a Task or an Instruction?
And let's not forget Aims and Targets*

A discussion about objectivity might look a bit out of place in this book; however, experience has shown that people at all levels in organisations can be quite poor at describing what the organisation is actually about.

For example, I worked for seven years in an organisation without being truly aware of its real purpose; it was only after they fired me and I reflected that I began to see the deeper purpose and objective of that organisation.

So if you are clear in your thinking and clear with objectivity it makes it a lot easier to understand what is behind a job advert, to craft an appropriate approach and to better manage the interview.

This appendix takes an academic stance, so please feel free to skip it if it seems a bit heavy

The reason you will be hired is to help an organisation achieve its particular commercial objectives; regrettably those objectives aren't always evident or clearly spelled out and can become easily confused, for example with tasks or targets.

The thoughts below relate to a commercial situation where transactions occur and those transactions change the situation for one or more of the stakeholders in the business.

Preamble

The classic way of examining or developing a business is by means of the journey:

- Vision
- Mission
- Objective
- Strategy
- Tactics

When using this approach it is normally straightforward to work with a business owner or executive director to clarify the fundamental purpose of the organisation and signpost ways to strengthen the relationship with their stakeholders by improved ways to manage their customers.

A currently unsatisfactory situation

There is quite a broad view that anything made SMART becomes an objective – fine, but can lead to trivialisation and confusion between objective, task and instruction. SMART refers to:

• Specific – relates to one thing only

• Measurable – can be quantified

• Achievable – there is sufficient market available

• Realistic – the capability and resources exist or can be acquired

• Time-bound – specific dates and deadlines can be ascribed

An example of a SMART statement might be: "*Your position demands that you have cleared your desk by 4:30 every evening.*" This is a situation that actually meets the SMART requirements – if that measurement is an absence of something (stuff on the desk top).

However, this demand fails to deliver anything commercially worthwhile to any of the organisation's stakeholders.

Getting to the commercial objective

The prime responsibility of a business is to deliver (usually financial) benefit to its shareholders – so far, so good – yet that financial benefit must be wrested from the hands of the organisation's customers by delivering something that customer needs or wants; normally in the form of a benefit.

As noted earlier, benefits are both tangible (e.g. to save money) and intangible (e.g. to give someone confidence) and it is generally recognised that the pulling power of the intangible benefit is twice that of the tangible one.

For example I took one of my suppliers through the Vision, Mission, Objective, Strategy, Tactics journey for his business, with some changes for commercial reasons:

• Vision – private to him and kept confidential

• Mission – To increase turnover by increasing the number of people who benefit from his service

• SMART Objective (for the business) – based on sustainable growth
  • Specific – To Increase net margin by 50% within one year
  • Measurable – By tripling the number of items produced each year

- Achievable – By confirming there is sufficient market for the increased service
- Realisable – By using existing facilities with one extra (affordable) employee
- Time-bound – Starting in March 2015

- Strategy – Again confidential to the business

A reminder about benefits

A customer will enter into a transaction in order to gain some sort of advantage or benefit and the business that provides the benefit normally expects to receive something in return. The most common transaction is to trade a benefit for that customer's money which can be returned to the shareholders.

Benefits come in two basic varieties:

- Tangible – can be critically measured when decreasing as well as when increasing, turnover is an example where incremental changes are readily identified.

- Intangible – difficult to measure and most evident when they fail, trust is an example where confidence in another party may be normally high, but when broken becomes non-existent.

Over 70% of the reason to buy is intangible – the transaction will make the recipient feel better in some way with improved confidence, reassured or peace of mind.

However, most purchases need to be justified – normally on tangible grounds with how much improvement this new thing will bring about.

The dimensions of change generally follow those that begin to define benefits:

- Increase
- Improve
- Reduce
- Remove
- Save
- Solve

Whereby, if our objective will deliver benefit better than the competition's offering we have identified the Measurable dimension of the SMART objective.

Delivering the intangible benefit is becoming recognised as increasingly important and statistically quantified in aspects such as brand strength where, some thirty years ago, there were attempts to quantify intangibles such as goodwill – which is now embodied in the Financial Reporting Standards.

Developing a more satisfactory objective

Many of the intangible benefits can be measured by sampling to give a statistical result e.g. to raise our average perceived brand strength from 5.2 to 5.4 on a scale of 1-7.

The intangible deliverable is actually increased confidence in the brand by investors (one of the stakeholders) who should continue to invest in the business.

The tangible benefits lend themselves naturally to measurement, either as real figures e.g. to increase turnover by £10m or by calculable ratios such as to improve the Return on Assets by 1.5%.

With this in mind, the SMART objective (for the market) now lends itself to:

- Specific – Which benefit and to which stakeholder(s).

- Measurable – How much extra impact will that benefit deliver, and to whom.

- Achievable – Are there enough customers to deliver that volume of benefit to.

- Realistic – That we have the means to not only deliver that increased amount of benefit but also to reach out to that number of customers.

- Time-bound – how long it will take to complete the job (note in the earlier example, this was linked to the Specific criterion).

Moving through the organisation

This clarification of the corporate objective can now inform and direct activities for departments, teams and individuals which provides a clue as to how you will position yourself with regard to the opportunity you are applying for.

It also aligns closely with Will Schutz' findings whose research into inter-personal dynamics in the 1950s identified three stages for a team to go through to achieve top performance, these being:

- Having an objective common to all.

- Having responsibility <u>with</u> authority.

- Having open relationships with peers and colleagues.

Each criterion builds on the one before.

On to the SMART task

I argue that tasks can also be made SMART especially where they relate to someone else delivering a benefit, for example one such task to ensure adequate supply of material to ensure the benefits are delivered might be:

- Specific – To maintain supplies of a particular compound.

- Achievable – To a specified grade, or from several approved sources.

- Realisable – Below a particular price plus a back-up supplier.

- Measurable – Between 500g and 1.5Kg always in stock.

- Time-bound – As monitored on a weekly basis.

And the SMART instruction

Where an activity or requirement is made SMART but does not impact on the delivery of a benefit e.g. "Your objective is to have cleared your desk by 4:30 every evening." This is a situation that actually meets the SMART requirements – but is in fact an instruction, and as such, might be open to challenge as wasteful or diversionary.

There are many other examples which include: the Monday morning meeting and correctly completed outdated paperwork.

As an instruction, with little apparent relevance, the person receiving the instruction may well display one example of Newtonian mechanics in that it will be met with an equal and opposite reaction. This does little for productivity, objectivity or the delivery of appropriate and meaningful benefits.

A bit of a problem at the top

Sadly, few of the senior members of an organisation get to a position of such clarity – at least publicly; and if they do, it tends to stay within the confines of their elite group, leading to a degree of puzzlement as to why customers complain, shareholders aren't serviced and the workforce are incapable of absorbing instructions, often delivered through osmosis.

If senior people were a bit clearer, focused and communicative, many organisations would be more sustainable, profitable and blame free – it would also help guide the person applying for a post to ensure relevance and compatibility.

In Summary

SMART is a great acronym but is often used without sufficient thought and application. In business it can be equally applied to objectives, tasks and instructions and lead to some confusion of purpose by the people within the business, and uncertainty for those applying for advertised posts.

- As an objective, it defines the delivery of a benefit.
- As a task, it recognises things to be done to help others to deliver that benefit.
- As an instruction, its purpose might be challenged and the activity discarded, changed or simplified where appropriate.

As an interviewee or applicant you should be prepared to ask for sufficient clarity as to what the organisation is actually about, the benefits it delivers and what will be your particular SMART position within it.

About the Author

STEVE MULLINS

BSc (Hons.) BSc, FIC, CMC, FRSA, MCIM (Chartered Marketer)
Steve graduated in life sciences and ecology – good disciplines for big-picture thinking, he started his career with well known blue-chip companies: Mars, Grand Metropolitan and Gallaher. As an independent consultant he has worked with organisations as diverse as Medium and Small enterprises in addition to corporations such as BT and HSBC.

After more than twenty years in blue chip organisations he has some twenty five years experience in self-employment; he works as a mentor, consultant and strategist with practical experience in outplacement having been outplaced himself, so knows both sides of the desk.

He has supported redundancy programmes with a number of major organisations. Successes have included more than 95% of people finding a new job within three months of redundancy, or were billing if self-employed.

Steve has also published, appeared on BBC Local Radio, is a Programme Director for CMI Management Training and provides training in New Product Development and Marketing.

Terms of Use and Disclaimers

1. You must not:

1.a Publish, republish, sell, license, sub-license, rent, transfer, broadcast, distribute or redistribute this publication or any part of this publication by any means whether electronic or physical.

1.b Edit, modify, adapt or alter this publication or any part of this publication.

1.c Use this publication or any part of this publication in any way that is unlawful or in breach of any person's legal rights under any applicable law, or in any way that is offensive, indecent, discriminatory or otherwise objectionable.

1.d Use this publication, or any part of this publication to compete with us, or for any other commercial purpose.

1.e Delete, obscure or remove any copyright notices and other proprietary notices.

2. This is not advice

2.a This publication contains information and ideas about ways to look for a new position; this information is not advice and should not be treated as such.

2.b You must not rely on the information in this publication as an alternative to legal or professional advice from an appropriately qualified practitioner.

2.c You should not delay seeking legal advice, disregard legal advice, commence or discontinue any legal action because of information in this publication.

3. Fitness for purpose

3.a Whilst Ascot Associates Ltd. has endeavoured to ensure that all information is correct, Ascot Associates Ltd. cannot warrant or represent its completeness or accuracy, or fitness for purpose when used by a third party.

3.b Ascot Associates Ltd. do not warrant or represent that the use of this publication will lead to any particular outcome or result. In particular there is no guarantee that by using this publication you will obtain a new position or find your way into employment.

4. Limitations and exclusions of liability

4.a Ascot Associates Ltd. will not be liable for any damages, losses or consequential losses arising out of any action, event, or as a result of any action or event, occurring from your using the material in this publication.

5. Governing law

5.a This notice shall be governed by, and construed in accordance with, English law.

End Notes

(1) The American approach is that first is first, second is nowhere – never truer than in the job market.

(2) See Edgar Schein in Wikipedia for a more complete discussion.

(3) Adapted from *Trust Us, We're Experts* by Rampton & Stauber ISBN 1-58542-139-1. Page 291 ff.

(4) Personal values can be readily analysed to help identify the right organisation for you, to bring focus and to concentrate your energies. Everyone has different values which should be matched to those of the organisation; an analysis has been developed for this comparison by Ascot Associates Ltd.

(5) The scenario is that you're in an elevator with someone between floors and have the time to the next floor to gain their interest before the elevator doors open. It's how you would describe what you do to someone in 17 words or less and in a way that invites them to ask more about you.

One well known example is Coventry Cathedral when a visitor asked a stonemason what he was doing 'glorifying God' – led on to 'how are you doing that?' 'Creating beauty to remind people and provide a point of focus. A second stonemason was asked the same question and gave the response 'knocking lumps out of bits of stone'. Who would <u>you</u> rather spend time with and get to know?

(6) For an alternative approach please see *The Character of Organisations* by William Bridges ISBN 0-89106-149-5.

(7) Which is probably why so few applications get acknowledged.

(8) "Get the right people on the bus AND the wrong people off the bus" Page 199 of Jim Collins *Good to Great* ISBN 978-0-712-67609-0; it's also worth remembering that it's a good idea to get the right people in the right seats.

(9) Vince Golder – recognised as one of the top referral marketers, see his website at http://www.goldnetreferralmarketing.co.uk/

(10) For Peter Sellers' 1958 *Party Political Speech*: Follow this QR code.

There are also some cruel publications that report political speeches verbatim. Apparently in America during one presidential contest the **Daily Quaile** was a top seller.

(11) One very successful TV interviewer was Alan Whicker who explained that the secret of his success was to leave <u>just slightly</u> more time than expected before asking the follow-up question to the interviewee's answer – people don't like gaps in time (at least in the west) and rush to fill those gaps, sometimes with inappropriate, interesting or revealing material that wouldn't have been otherwise volunteered! So look out, it could happen to you.

Other Publications

The Story of Cash Flow
 - Thought to be the world's first folk tale based around management, and with a warning to the fledgling entrepreneur.
ISBN 978-0-9576340-2-2
  Steve Mullins

How Good Is My Glue?
 - Non-financial due diligence
Some of the things people might forget to ask
  Steve Mullins and Peter Ainsley

How Near Is My Cliff-Edge?
 - Five easy questions, ten searching answers
Challenging the purpose of your business
  Steve Mullins and Peter Ainsley

Strategy
 - Pitfalls and pathways
How to develop strategy
  Peter Ainsley and Steve Mullins

The People in the River
 - Twelve people you thought you knew
An alternative approach to people types
  Steve Mullins and Peter Ainsley

Referral Marketing
 - Turn your customers into your sales force
143 opportunities for new business
  Vince Golder and Steve Mullins

Be the Consummate Professional
 - Tips on how to maximise your professional
    credibility, status and success
Improve your status and business relationships
  Vince Golder and Steve Mullins

**All books and articles are available on
Kindle or through Amazon**

And each for about the price of a cup of High
  Street coffee! – ***Brilliant value***

Ethical Crisis Management
 - How any decision, delayed long enough, will
    seem to be a good one
ISSN 1741-5187 – The International Journal of
    Management & Decision Making, Vol. 6 2005,
    pp.372 - 381 – available only from the
    publishers

Steve Mullins can be contacted at:

E-mail steve.mullins@virgin.net

ISBN 9780957634039

9 780957 634039